THE ART AND SCIENCE OF RUNNING A CAR DEALERSHIP

MAX ZANAN

Copyright 2019 All rights reserved

ISBN: 9781691591329

TABLE OF CONTENTS

Foreword by Ted Ings v

Introduction
A Do Not Skip This Section ix
B Who Am I to Tell You What to Do? xi
C Distractions xiii

Body
1   Initial Walkaround 1
2   Initial Internet Walkaround 4
3   Mystery Shopping (Sales/BDC/F&I) 9
4   Mystery Shopping (Service/Parts) 13
5   Define Your Dealership 18
6   Understanding Organizational Culture 21
7   Employee Morale 25
8   Organizational Mission Statement 31
9   Building the Team 34
10 Defining Customer Experience (Walk-In) 37

11	Defining Customer Experience (BDC)	41
12	Defining Customer Experience (Service)	44
13	Defining Customer Service (Express Service)	46
14	Defining Customer Experience with Repairs and Recalls	49
15	Role of BDC in Defining Customer Experience in Service	52
16	Defining Customer Experience in Parts (1)	54
17	Defining Customer Experience in Parts (2)	56
18	Additional Profit Centers	58
19	Tire Sales	61
20	Detail Center	64
21	Customization	66
22	Selling F&I Products Online	68
23	Wholesale	70
24	Servicing Fleet Accounts	72
25	Dealer-Owned Prepaid Maintenance	74
26	Post-Sale F&I Product Follow-up	76
27	Dealer-Owned Subscriptions	78
28	Dealer-Owned Insurance Agency	81
29	Dealer-Owned Body Shop	83
30	Measuring Performance	85
31	Communication	89
32	Reviews	91
33	Relationships	93
34	Conclusion	95
35	References	97

FOREWORD BY TED INGS

I am honored and humbled that Max Zanan asked me to write the forward of his new book "The Art and Science of Running a Car Dealership."

I've been an admirer of Max's work for many years and have followed his career closely. This makes writing a forward for his third book both a privilege and a challenge because it is hard to encapsulate in so few paragraphs who Max is and what he has meant to the automotive industry. I could probably write a whole book on the subject!

Max is more than passionate about the car business. He is obsessed with it!

He will be the first to tell you that everything he has he owes to the automotive retail industry and it has made him what he is today. But besides what the car industry means to Max, I think it is important that we do not overlook the impact that he has had on the industry.

Max Zanan's insight and vision have helped many dealerships weather the storms of change and remain in business through challenging times. He has consulted with countless clients, highlighting their strengths and weaknesses and helping them develop a sustainable plan for the future.

Max, however, is not a fortune teller or magician, his insight is not gained by reading the stars or staring into a crystal ball but rather from hard work and years of experience.

Max grew up in the car business and worked in every department of the car dealership. He started as a salesperson and later worked as a sales manager, finance manager, general sales manager, service manager, and general manager, finally ending his automotive retail career running a group that broke multiple sales and gross profit records.

From there Max shifted his focus and began providing income development services through F&I products and later opened Total Dealership Compliance.

He now also provides training and dealership consulting services that focus on improving processes, customer services, and profitability.

During his many years in the industry, Max has seen trends come and go and he has also witnessed how dealerships that can't see the writing on the wall flounder and ultimately close their doors for good.

One of Max's many great qualities is that he always wants to share his insight and knowledge with other people and what better way to reach a large audience than through writing books. "The Art and Science of Running a Car Dealership" is Max's third book and his previous two books, "Perfect Dealership – Surviving the Digital Disruption" and "Car Business 101" are a must-read for anyone who wants to succeed in the automotive retail industry.

Max's extensive experience and long career in the automotive retail industry, as well as his work as a consultant for all aspects of dealership operations, means that he is ideally positioned to have unique insights into the future of the car business.

Max's first foray into the world of publishing, "Perfect Dealership – Surviving the Digital Disruption" was published in 2017 and is a wake-up call to the industry. It focuses on one of Max's great passions, helping dealerships around the country not only survive well into the future but also thrive.

"Perfect Dealership" offers general managers, dealer principles and everyone in the automotive retail industry insight into the future of the car retail but more than that it gives dealerships a concrete plan for transforming their businesses and surviving the digital disruption.

His second book, "Car Business 101 - #Crazy Sh*t Car Dealers Do." is also aimed at Dealer Principals, General Managers and employees rather than consumers. It looks at all the things that car dealers do wrong, why they don't work and what you should be doing instead. Both books take a close and critical look at the crossroads that has been reached by the automotive retail industry and where we go from here.

Through his writing, Max demonstrates how the mind of the consumer is changing and how the market is changing with them and he highlights the fact that companies that refuse to change will go out of business.

Max warns brick and mortar dealerships that if they do not adapt and alter the way that they interact with their customers, they will go the way of the dinosaur. But his focus is not just traditional dealerships, Max understands that the entire industry needs to do better and in order to win the respect of the consumer we have to aspire to excellence in every aspect of our business.

Not only does Max understand the automotive industry, but he also understands people and he knows that people, both customers, and employees, are the backbone of any successful business. Our customers have become savvier and are not afraid to ask for what they want and shop around until they find it.

Max is resolute in his opinion that customer satisfaction is the key to ensuring customer retention and he shares his invaluable advice on how to meet the customer's needs in every department.

But over and above customer satisfaction, Max emphasizes the importance of hiring the right people for the right positions because after all, it is these people who will deliver the high level of customer service that you require.

Being a car salesperson can no longer just be a job that pays the bills, it needs to become a respected career. To achieve this, dealerships need to offer people a clear career path with training and support for new hires.

Everyone in the dealership must have the opportunity to develop their skills and rise to the level of their innate ability. As an industry, we need to give our employees a future and not treat them as if they are disposable.

All these lessons are part of Max's writing and whether you are new to the automotive retail industry or an old hand, you can learn a lot about dealing with people from this stalwart of the automotive retail industry.

When you work in the car retail industry, many interesting people cross your path and you will learn various lessons from all of them, even if it is what not to do, but the really great people will challenge the way you think. They will open your eyes to a future that you may not have envisioned and Max Zanan is one of those great minds.

In my 40-year career in the retail industry, I have not met many people with Max's insight and understanding of what is truly both an art and a science.

Max can walk into a dealership and within 2-3 minutes know exactly whether it is a well-run machine or an accident waiting to happen. He truly "gets it" - which so few people in our industry presently do. Even more importantly, he identifies current and upcoming trends which will have a great impact on the future of retail, not just for the car industry but for other businesses as well.

Max is a clever, insightful and talented individual whose abilities and insights go far beyond the car industry. I am proud to call him a friend and mentor. Enjoy the book! It's great reading!"

A.
DO NOT SKIP THIS SECTION

THIS BOOK IS the pocket guide I wish I had when I first became a general manager of a Mitsubishi dealership in New York. Honestly, I am not the brightest star in the sky and made every mistake anyone could've possibly made.

Unfortunately, I see dealer principals/general managers/general sales managers making the same mistakes today. The only difference is the time and consequences of these mistakes. I got my first GM gig in 2004. That was in the beginning days of the Internet, before millennials joined the workforce, and way before any viable disrupters entered the market space. It was a lot easier to get away with mistakes then. I don't think you could get away with making the same mistakes now.

The stakes are too high. Automotive retail profit margins are tiny. According to the National Automobile Dealers Association (NADA), automotive net profit margin as of March 31, 2019 was merely 1.38 percent. As a result, every misstep makes it harder to stay in business.

The car business desperately needs better leadership skills, understanding of social media, inventory management, fixed operations, and so much more.

There is no educational barrier to the entry into car business, and there are only a handful of universities offering a major in car dealership general management, such as Liberty and Keiser. On top of that, only a tiny percentage of dealer principals and general managers attend the National Automobile Dealer Association University.

That means that a vast majority of general managers receive training on the job, even if we took business-related classes in college. The auto business is a different animal. General information will only carry you so far. That is exactly why general managers make the same mistakes year after year.

My goal is to break this vicious cycle and provide as much information as possible to ensure that automotive retail survives the disruptions we are witnessing today.

We need to be ready for the next generation of car buyers, people who are more computer savvy and not afraid to search for better deals. According to surveys, 80 percent of millennials plan to buy a vehicle in the next five years. In fact, millennials worldwide will buy about 40 percent of all vehicles in the next decade.

At the same time, they spend an average of 17 hours on line before going to a dealership.

Are you ready for them?

* * *

Beyond advice in this booklet, you'll find a reference section at the end of the book that lists all reputable vendors that you might want to reach out to.

B.
WHO AM I TO TELL YOU WHAT TO DO?

I have been in car business since 2001. It's the only thing I know. I started selling cars then and was absolutely terrible because zero training was provided – unless watching the movie Suckers is considered training.

Eventually, it all came together. I have held almost every position in a car dealership, including salesman, sales manager, finance manager, general sales manager, finance director, service manager, general manager and platform president. In recent years, I transitioned from retail into operational consulting, F&I income development and compliance.

I have seen every aspect of the business and have done it myself.

Being able to objectively look at automotive retail from many different angles helps me provide value to my dealer clients. My hope is that this book will make your life easier and your dealership more profitable.

I love car business and want to do everything in my power to preserve the franchise model. However, we need to get better at running car dealerships, and we need to do it quickly. Competition is coming at us from every side.

C.
DISTRACTIONS

This book is about day-to-day operations of a car dealership, not about fantasies being pushed by auto makers and media.

Do not be overly concerned about:

1. Electric cars: Total fantasy. There is no real demand for these cars; not to mention the fact that there is no charging infrastructure. The only way electric cars become a reality is if federal government legislates combustion engine out of existence.

2. Autonomous cars: We are years away. Still, they are coming. The auto industry plans to invest at least $100 billion in the technology. In 2018, the U.S. Department of Transportation updated guidelines and reduced federal oversight. The public remains skeptical. A recent study by research firm J.D. Power and Associates and the National Association of Mutual Insurance Companies found that 40 percent of Americans said they "would never ride" in a fully automated vehicle. The logic is obvious: Are you willing to let go of your steering wheel? Let's be honest

– the answer is, "No way." Of course, a younger generation who grows up with self-driving cars may respond differently.

3. Rideshare mobility: Science fiction. It is not cost effective now to use Uber/Lyft for all your transportation needs. Do not forget that those companies subsidize every ride. At some point, they will have to raise their prices in order to show a profit. They are not available everywhere and have limitations. What about a simple convenience of having a golf bag or a gym bag in your trunk?

Do not be distracted by these possibilities because it might have a paralyzing effect on your focus on things that you can actually control. A lot of bad things are happening which require your attention:

1. Unacceptable transaction time
2. Poor customer service
3. Terrible service retention
4. Sky-high employee turnover
5. Non-existent digital retail

Let's jump into the nitty-gritty and offer ways to help you improve your dealership.

1
INITIAL WALKAROUND

WHETHER YOU JUST bought a dealership or got a promotion to be a general manager, the first thing you must do is a thorough walkaround of the facility and a complete investigation of your website. The key is to look at what you have, not as automotive retail professional but as a consumer.

Below is the checklist that should help you:

EXTERIOR

1. Is overall appearance of the dealership welcoming to the walk-in and drive-in traffic? There is a lot to unpack here: from ease of parking to having a blowup gorilla that sends a clear signal that the place is stuck in 1980s.

2. Is there valet parking or clearly marked customer parking? New York city dealers must provide valet parking, but a lot of them fail to mention it on their websites.

3. Are there are signs in the window with lowball lease payments? Customers are not stupid; they know these are bogus numbers.

4. Are sales people standing outside smoking? All these visual clues send a signal to the general public and help determine if they will either visit your dealership or not.

INTERIOR

1. Is overall appearance of the showroom welcoming? Bright open spaces and modern furniture makes a difference.
2. Is there a front desk?
3. Is the facial expression and body language of the receptionist friendly and welcoming?
4. Is the showroom clean, well-lit and modern?
5. Is it easy to identify employees via dress code and nametags?
6. Are modern desktop/laptop computers on sales peoples' desks?
7. Are vehicles on the showroom floor open?
8. Is music playing or you can hear a pin drop? You don't want your dealership to resemble a ghost town.
9. Is there coffee/water readily available?
10. Are prices clearly displayed on each vehicle? Not MSRP but real sale prices. We are getting closer and closer where car dealers will have no choice but switch to one-price model because of digital retail. You simply cannot have one price online and a negotiated price in the showroom.
11. Is service customer-waiting area clean and comfortable with modern furniture, food, drinks, reading materials, computers, WIFI?
12. Are there any additional services that customers can take advantage of while waiting, including haircuts, manicures, pedicures, etc.

13. Do service and parts employees wear uniforms and nametags?
14. Is there a retail shop? Is it well-stocked? Are there prices on all items for sale? Is there a salesperson/cashier present?
15. Are the technicians' OEM certificates on the wall?
16. Is there a salesperson present to assist with the vehicle exchange program?
17. Are there are signs promoting any available additional services, such as detail, tires, customization, bodywork, etc.?

Car business is not nuclear physics. If you master the basics, your dealership will be very successful. This checklist should help you put your finger on the pulse and make simple changes that will have a positive effect on customers and employees.

These days, customers are used to clean and modern showrooms – think Apple computer stores – and transparent pricing – another Amazon innovation. So, if you think that it is acceptable to operate as if you are stuck in the last century, customers will punish you.

Amazing customer service, a frictionless sales process and a welcoming environment will separate you from the competition.

2
INITIAL INTERNET WALKAROUND

RESEARCH SHOWS THAT about 86 percent of customers who visit your showroom or service department first went to your website. I think the real number is close to 99%. As a result, you need to look at the dealership's web presence as a customer. Remember that first impressions are everything.

Don't assume that if you can use it, anyone can. Visit your site and pretend you are looking for a car. Go to your competitors' sites. Go to other businesses. See what they are doing. Pick up any ideas you can to improve the experience for your customers and to identify any potential snags.

Below is the checklist that should help you:

1. Google the name of your dealership.
2. How many Google reviews does the dealership have? The more reviews the better. Consumers trust reviews more so than referrals. How many stars? Anything below 4.9 star rating is a failure.

3. How many Yelp reviews does the dealership have? How many stars?
4. Keep going down the list: Cars.com, Autotrader.com, CarGurus.com, DealerRater, etc.
5. Read reviews to understand what the customers' concerns are and see if the concerns are being answered.
6. See if customer complaints are aimed at sales, F&I or the service department.
7. When you look at the 1st page of Google, see if the star ratings is below 4.5. If so, a lot of customers will keep looking for a dealership with higher reviews.
8. Does the dealership website look generic? If so, then you will find it harder to stand out from competition. OEMs have facility upgrade requirements that could cost millions of dollars. It's a lot less expensive to upgrade a website. In reality, most dealerships' websites need to be upgraded on a regular basis to improve digital retail.
9. Are the forms simple and easy to use? Regardless of the request, such as scheduling a test drive or booking a service appointment, the forms should have limited options. That's saves time and increases chances the customer will follow through.
10. Is there a clear "why buy from us" message? Is it on the home page? Is there a video recorded by the dealer principal? There is nothing more powerful than the business owner explaining to existing and potential customers why this dealership is different.
11. Are there customers' reviews right on the dealership website?
12. Are sale prices clearly displayed? If you see MSRP or ask customers to call for a price or claim prices are "too low to show," you have a lot of work to do.

13. Is there a dealership YouTube channel?
14. Is there a dealership Facebook page?
15. Is there an Instagram dealership page?
16. Is there a LinkedIn dealership page?
17. How frequently social media pages are updated?
18. Do these pages have compelling content and customer engagements?
19. How much of a deal can a customer do online?
20. Is there a Better Business accreditation right on the website?
21. Is there information about F&I products, terms and coverage? Are there sample contracts for the customers to review?
22. Is there a trade-in appraisal tool?
23. Can a customer go online and schedule a test drive?
24. Can a customer buy parts online?
25. Can a customer schedule a service appointment on line?
26. Are service loaners available? If so, how can a customer request one?
27. Does the dealership offer home delivery?
28. What is the radius for free home delivery of a new vehicle?
29. Does the dealership offer a return policy?
30. What are the business hours? Is the service department open late, on weekends or 24 hours?
31. Does service department offer home pick-up and drop-off service?
32. Does the dealership offer car rentals or loaners?

E-commerce is part of our everyday life. As a result, consumers have certain expectations when they visit your dealership's website. Make sure that your website is easy to navigate, informative and, most importantly, transactional. This is the time to make a real investment into your website instead of wasting millions of dollars on facility upgrades.

1. Any website design should be clear of distractions with eye-catching navigation tools. Customers presented with too many options have problems making decisions. You want to reduce frustration and ease passage to wherever your customer wants to go on your site. The less thinking, the better.

2. Provide an on-line calculator. Customers will want to know the exact cost of a car and monthly payments. Anything you can do to facilitate the process increases likelihood of a sale.

3. Be sure you include multiple ways to reach the same destination. In a study of auto dealer websites, 76 percent of participants rated as the most important aspect "the website makes it easy to find what I want."

4. Don't hesitate to let the website reflect the personality of our dealership. If you are trying to be hip, then your website should reflect that approach. That's true if you want to be sophisticated, humorous or any other option. The approach should connect to your audience, as outlined in your business plan.

5. Limit the forms. No one wants to fill out paperwork inside the dealership. Give a customer a chance to do most of it at home rather than spend excessive time in the dealership.

6. Use visuals. We all prefer to see something for ourselves. Show off your cars. Include videos and still pictures. The videos don't have to be ads. They can show everyday people unloading a car, driving over rough terrain or whatever

aspect you want to highlight. Throw in a few cute cats and dogs, and you have something to attract customers and hold their attention.

7. Link your website to social media sites. Make it easy for a customer to send an image of a new car to friends and family.

8. Be sure your website images reflect the dealership. Walk people through the front door. Have the receptionist greet them via the video. Introduce various departments. When customers do come to the showroom, the familiarity will make them feel more comfortable.

The more your website resembles Amazon's the better. Most of us use Amazon daily, and we are trained to look for reviews, smooth checkout process and home delivery. No need to reinvent the wheel. If you can't beat them, imitate them.

3
MYSTERY SHOPPING (SALES/BDC/F&I)

AFTER YOUR INITIAL walkaround, it is time look under the hood by mystery shopping in your dealership. Not many dealers mystery (also called "secret") shop their businesses because they are afraid of what they are going to find.

In my opinion, mystery shopping is the most effective approach to discovering and fixing inefficiencies. When I am talking about mystery shopping, I mean the entire process from calling to visiting the showroom, going through F&I, and delivery. Same goes for service. As a customer, go from initial contact to bringing the car in for service and getting the work done. Do the same thing for parts. You get the idea.

There are companies that specialize in mystery shopping services, and you should definitely use them on the ongoing basis. However, if possible, try to do the first mystery shopping yourself.

Below is the checklist that should help you mystery shop the sales, BDC and F&I departments:

1. Call the dealership in order to gauge the friendliness of the person who is answering the phone. First impressions matter, an idea I will continue to emphasize.
2. If instead of the live person, there is an automated system, determine if it is easy to navigate and if it does what it is supposed to do. For example, what happens when you press 1 for sales? Do you actually get transferred to sales?
3. If a receptionist answers the phone and you ask to speak to sales, how long is the hold time?
4. What is the hold time if you ask to speak to the finance manager?
5. Is voicemail available? If so, then leave a message to determine the callback time.
6. When a sales person or the finance manager answers the phone, do they introduce themselves?
7. Is the sales person willing to provide the exact sales price/lease payment on the phone?
8. Does the sale person follow a script and ask for an appointment?
9. What is the response time for an online lead?
10. Is it an automatic responder or a real response?
11. Does an email response contain exact sale price/lease payment or is it vague?
12. Is there an up system or is it an open floor?
13. Does the sales person understand the necessary steps to the sale?
14. Does the sales person have the necessary product knowledge? Product knowledge is key. Sales people must know what makes their vehicles unique and how their cars compare to competition.

15. Is the sales price/lease payment clearly displayed on the buyer's order?
16. How many trips to the podium to speak to the manager did it take to make the deal?
17. Who appraised the trade?
18. Were you there for the trade appraisal?
19. Did the used car manager conducting the appraisal point out certain facts, such as scratches, chipped paint, etc.?
20. Is there an insurance broker on premises to help get the best quote possible?
21. How long did it take to make the deal?
22. How long did it take to get into F&I?
23. Was the finance manager professionally dressed?
24. Were there any compliance certificates in the finance office?
25. Did finance manager use an electronic menu?
26. Did finance manager clearly explain every product on the menu?
27. Were there any visual aids in the finance office?
28. Did the finance manager explain Truth in Lending disclosure on the retail installment contract?
29. Were F&I products sold in ethical manner?
30. Was the vehicle delivered clean?
31. Did the sales person explain all features of the vehicle and how to use it?
32. Was an encore delivery offered? Vehicles are becoming more complicated every year. There are more features than ever, and it is hard for an average consumer to digest all

of the information on delivery. Encore delivery allows the customer to come back a few days later to go over the car again.

33. Was the OEM customer satisfaction survey clearly explained?

34. How much time did it take to buy a car? Timing is everything. Anything over an hour and half will negatively impact customer satisfaction and gross profit. You should really strive for one hour or less.

Once you mystery shop the entire sales process, you will see the inner workings of the organization and its inefficiencies. This approach will help you formulate the strategy to improve the process and make it more customer friendly.

If you don't hire an outside firm, there are several ways you can mystery shop your dealership.

1. Have a colleague videotape a shopping experience. Doing it discretely is the best way. The customer should know about the filming, but your staff should not.

2. Have shoppers attempt to buy a car on line and report their experiences.

3. Listen in to phone calls made by customers to your staff. Many are recorded these days anyway.

4. Shop competitors and see what they are doing, both good and bad. You may learn something very helpful.

4
MYSTERY SHOPPING (SERVICE/PARTS)

AS I MENTIONED before, not a lot of car dealers mystery shop their dealerships because they are afraid to learn what really goes on in their business under the theory that ignorance is bliss.

Even fewer car dealers mystery shop their service and parts departments because they don't understand the fixed operations side of the business. Only three percent of dealer principals, partners, and general managers have a fixed ops background.

It is increasingly harder to make money selling cars. You absolutely must understand and focus on service and parts in order to survive this margin compression. NADA research shows that only 56 percent of a dealer's income these days comes from the sale of new cars. The rest has to come from somewhere.

Service and parts is not that complicated, and every dealer principal and general manager must understand it. The point of this exercise is to see it from the customers' perspective.

Below is the checklist that should help you with basics:

1. Are service hours convenient?
2. Can you make a service appointment online?
3. Do you need to make an appointment for an oil change? It is absolutely unacceptable to wait for an appointment for an oil change. Same day is the only acceptable option.
4. If you have to call to make a service appointment, how long does it take to get transferred and to schedule the appointment?
5. Is there an email confirmation of an appointment?
6. Could you cancel or modify appointment time via email?
7. When is the next available appointment?
8. Was the loaner offered?
9. Once you pulled into the service drive, was your presence acknowledged right away with a smile and eye contact?
10. Did service advisor come out to greet you?
11. Was service advisor professionally dressed and friendly?
12. Did service advisor succeed at building rapport?
13. Did service advisor conduct an active walkaround?
14. Did service advisor use a tablet?
15. Did service advisor make an attempt to upsell from the walkaround, including an estimate for body work, new tires, detailing, etc.?
16. Was wheel alignment/tire thread checked? Was Hunter equipment available? Hunter machines provide a third-party validation that the work is needed.
17. Did service advisor know why you were coming in?

18. Did service advisor check service history?
19. If you decided to wait, how long before service advisor come back with Multi-Point Vehicle Inspection filled out by a technician?
20. If you decided to leave, was a loaner offered? If not, was Uber or Lyft offered?
21. If you decided to leave, how long before service advisor contacted you to go over Multi-Point Vehicle Inspection?
22. How were you contacted – by phone, text, email, video?
23. Could you authorize additional work via email or text?
24. If you declined suggested work, was it recorded on the repair order?
25. Was 0 percent APR repair order financing available? Were there point of sale materials? Did the service advisor bring it up?
26. Did service advisor notify you of the progress and the time you can pick up your vehicle?
27. Did service advisor conduct an active delivery of the vehicle?
28. Was the vehicle returned clean?
29. Were you offered a discount/credit for future service if the vehicle wasn't returned on time?
30. Was home pick-up and delivery offered for the future service work?
31. If you were there for an oil change, how long did it take? Anything over 30 minutes ensures that probability of the customer coming back in the future is slim to none.
32. How was the cash-out process? Cashier or advisor?

33. Was a loyalty program offered to you? For example, every third oil change is free.
34. Was there a vehicle exchange department in the service drive?
35. Were there oil change part kits in the retail shop?
36. Were you asked to prepay a special-order part?
37. Did you see a tire display?
38. How long did it take to get transferred to parts?
39. Did the parts counter person attempt to take a credit card payment over the phone?
40. Were you able to buy parts from the dealership's website? If so, were you emailed a shipping confirmation?
41. Were you emailed a coupon for future parts purchases?

Here are several suggested ways to improve profits via the Parts Department.

1. Don't discount parts.
2. Buy parts from other dealers.
3. Use the express service to promote common parts, such as filters, brake pads and tires.
4. Be competitive in pricing common items. Consumers shop around for those products.
5. Keep a list of lost sales because a part was not available. That will help you restock your inventory. Do a daily inventory to be sure important supplies are readily available.
6. Have customer pre-pay for special order parts. Keep the customer informed of the status of the order and notify the customer immediately when the part arrives.

As you can see, there is a lot to digest, and we are just scratching the surface. Now that you have customers' perspective, you can start thinking about making it better.

5
DEFINE YOUR DEALERSHIP

IN ORDER FOR you to accomplish your goals, you need to understand what kind of dealership you have. Are you happy with its current place in the market or do you want to change direction? Let's start by asking some basic questions:

1. Is this a new or used car dealership?
2. Is the emphasis on new car sales or used car sales? Remember that golden ratio is 1:1 – one new car sale for each used car sale. What is the ratio now?
3. How does the dealership rank in the zone, district, and nation?
4. Are you happy with current ranking?
5. Is the dealership profitable?
6. Where is the profit coming from – new car sales, used car sales, parts and service?

7. What kind of culture does the dealership have? Is this a low profit/high volume dealership? Or high profit/low volume?

8. Is the dealership an active corporate citizen in the community?

Once you answer these questions it should be easier to define what you need to accomplish and how to get there. Understanding the current position of the organization should help you outline strategy to move forward.

Begin by identifying your dealership's position in the market. Where are your competitors, both in distance and success? What will you need to do to compete with them and differentiate yourself?

Identify your customers. If you are selling luxury automobiles, you are going after a different audience than someone marketing low-priced imports. Once you pinpoint your customer base, consider the best ways to reach them. Would they be enticed by drawings, prizes or a free service, such as an oil change?

Then, decide what image do you want to present to the public: Sophisticated? Less expensive? Casual shopping? And so on. That depends on your audience and your environment. You are trying to differentiate yourself and appeal to your customer base. All of your marketing needs to emphasize that message.

A business plan must be part of the process. Keep it short and avoid jargon. A business plan needs to be regularly reviewed and updated as events and conditions change. No one wants to read hundreds of pages filled with unfamiliar words.

Business plans have several required elements.

1. Opportunity: Explain what you are selling and identify your target market.

2. Execution: Explain how you plan to reach that market. This section needs to set benchmarks to indicate when

you have reached the expected results as well as your sales and marketing plans.

3. Team: This section details the dealership's organizational plan as well as requirements for employees needed to fill the various roles.

4. Financial: This section describes funding, monthly sales and revenue projections for the first 12 months, and then annual projections for the next three to five years.

6
UNDERSTANDING ORGANIZATIONAL CULTURE

DEVELOPING A GREAT team that enjoys coming to work is one of the most important goals you should have. Not all employees that you've inherited will continue, especially if you are planning to institute a variety of changes. People do not like change. Before you start making changes, you need to understand existing culture of the organization. The only way to accomplish this is to interview as many employees as possible.

Below is the list of questions I would ask:

1. Does the dealership have a well-defined mission statement? If so, do you know what it is?

2. Is there a code of ethics that all employees should follow?

3. Are there well-defined corporate values?

4. Is there a well-defined path to promotion?
5. Is this a career or just a job?
6. Are all departments working towards the same well-defined goal? Or does every department have its own agenda?
7. When was the last time there was an interdepartmental meeting to get everybody on the same page?
8. What would you change about the organization?
9. Do you like working here?

I am not naïve and know that not all employees will volunteer a lot of information. As a result, this is the best time to set-up a whistle blower hotline. Car dealerships are small business that operate in confined spaces. As such, it is hard for some employees to blow a whistle on a colleague because of the negative impact it might have on them and their coworkers.

A whistle blower hotline is an 800-number administered by a third party. Employees make anonymous calls to report issues and potential fraud. The third party assigns a case number to each call and forwards the information to you to investigate. Once you complete the investigation, you forward the resolution to the whistle blower hotline which, in turn, contacts the employee.

Every publicly traded company is required to have a whistle blower hotline because it helps protect the company. Every dealership should have one as well because this kind of anonymous reporting system will allow you to take corrective action before issues escalate. It will also provide valuable insight into the organization in the beginning of your tenure.

Check out www.DealershipFraudHotline.com The cost is only $365 per year. That's a small price to pay to find out what is really going on in your organization.

Next step is to have a senior management meeting to outline your vision. This is the time when leadership skills are really important. This is the time to inspire and motivate.

Below are the pillars and goals of a successful organization:

1. Improve employee morale and reduce turnover.
2. Improve customer satisfaction.
3. Improve customer retention.
4. Increase profits.

Each organization will accomplish these goals differently and there is no one right methods; however, some fundamentals are universal. Goals must be specific, measurable, achievable and timely. They must also reflect long-term achievements.

There are three basic types of goals:

1. Time: These can be long-term or short-term.
2. Focus: These goals affect others. For example, if you want to double sales, for example, you will have to improve training. That way the main goal affects other aspects of the dealership.
3. Topic: These affect individuals, such as making more money, getting a college degree or a promotion. Such goals can be personal, career-related or both.

To achieve any goal, you need objectives. These are the step-by-step increments leading to the completed goal. There are five recognized steps in any such plan.

1. Name: Identify exactly what your goal is.
2. Measurable: How will you measure that you have achieved your goal?
3. Action: What must be done to reach that goal? List every steps. You can check them off as you near your goal.
4. Assistance: Whose help will you need to reach your goal? Does your boss need to be flexible in scheduling? Do you need a loan?

5. Calendar: How much time are you allotting to achieve your goal?

For example, if you want to obtain an advanced college degree, your first objective will be to pick a subject, then the institution, then enroll, obtain good grades and, finally, in the allotted time, reach your goal.

Detailed plans like this should be part of every goal.

7
EMPLOYEE MORALE

EMPLOYEE MORALE WILL make or break your organization. Happy employees are motivated, go the extra mile, provide awesome customer service, and are the best advocates for your business.

Motivated employees, communicate better, understand their colleagues' strengths and weaknesses; have respect and support one another. They also motivate each other and, in many ways, police activities because they want the system to work.

How do you build a team?

1. **Set organizational goals**

    This establishes the vision that each employee can appreciate and work towards. Employees who understand and invest in the goals of the dealership are willing partners.

2. **Set team goals**

    Dealerships typically are divided into departments. Employees must know and understand what the goals of their department are. To accomplish them, they will have to work together. As with any goal, you need to have performance indicators to let employees know when they have moved closer to the final goal. Cross-training ensures that employees understand the various jobs in the department and can appreciate how each person is needed to reach the described departmental goal.

3. **Reward**

    Understandably, salespeople mostly work on a commission, a process not available for accounting, service and other areas. However, all departments should be eligible for bonuses when goals are met. That doesn't eliminate individual recognition but helps ensure that everyone works together to achieve a goal and is rewarded as a team for success. You want to reduce the "what is in for me?" syndrome and replace it with rewards for how well employees contribute to the team.

4. **Competition**

    Encourage teams to participate in friendly competition in events such as walk-a-thons. The idea is not to give financial rewards, but plaques and other incentives that encourage bonding within a unit. Social activities outside of work continue the bonding process. According to an MIT study, team performance can jump as much as 35 percent when members socialize outside work. Anything you can do to help team members get to know each other better will boost morale and performance. That includes eating lunch together, going places as a group, working on volunteer projects or even taking walks together during break time.

5. **Cross-Functional Teams**

    You also don't want to isolate teams. Create team of employees from different departments to work on broader dealership goals, such as improving customer experience, upgrading technology or developing new employee incentives.

A cross-team could interview candidates to help you gauge how the potential employee might fit into the corporate culture. At the same time, everyone learns how other departments function, improving communication and overall cooperation.

6. **Train**

    To accomplish your goal of building a team, you will have to have department managers who understand the processes involved. Just as you have learned how to build a team, your managers may need the same training. That's especially true of a manager who is self-motivated and can't understand why an employee is not.

7. **Measure**

    Employees need to know how they are doing in achieving goals. That encourages them to work harder to reach the prescribed level.

How do you ensure that you have the right team in place?

Once you met with department heads to present your vision, you have to meet with the entire organization to do the same thing. Ask employees if they are willing to accept the changes and be team players. Remember, people do not like change. Some veteran employees might not be eager to adapt to any changes. I would even offer to pay a $500 bonus for each employee that decides to leave. Trust me: this is a small price to pay to get rid of individuals who will work to undermine your plans for the dealership.

What are the building blocks of employee morale? There are multiple books dedicated to this subject that you should read. My favorite is *Uncontainable: How Passion, Commitment, and Conscious Capitalism Built a Business Where Everyone Thrives* by Kip Tindell. Kip Tindell was the chairman and CEO of The Container Store, one of the most profitable retailers in America. Employee satisfaction there is through the roof, and the company enjoys extremely low turnover.

Communication is the foundation of employee morale. As a dealer principal or general manager, you must be accessible and have an open-door policy. Employees should know that they can speak to you about their issues and concerns. In addition, a good leader is capable of communicating organizational goals and milestones. Having regular meetings is key. I am a big fan of having meetings with department heads and separate meetings with employees. This way, nothing gets lost in translation.

Most people want to have a career and be a part of something great. It is your job to paint a promising picture and have powerful goals. For example, my goal when I was a general manager was to be the highest volume and most profitable Mitsubishi dealership in the country. It seemed impossible at first, but once the team bought into the idea, we got it done in 13 months.

Providing training for new hires and ongoing training for existing employees are also keys to improving employee morale. As you know, there are no educational barriers in the car business – we hire pretty much anybody with a pulse. So, it is your responsibility to train employees. It all starts with proper onboarding of new hires. They need to understand your culture, values, policies, procedures, etc. before they can start performing their duties. Not a lot of dealers invest in training. Then they wonder why the employee turnover is so high.

Training means different things to different people. Some dealers think that basic product knowledge and sales training is enough. I strongly disagree with that. How about a basic English 101 course so employees know how to write a professional email? Employees who do not know basic email etiquette reflect badly on your business, and that's a sure way to lose credibility. Would you buy a $50,000 car from someone who can't spell or put together proper, grammatically correct email? How about a course on body language? Remember that great salespeople are not born, they are made. It is your job to make them.

Moreover, there has to be a clear path for career growth. For example, your sales personnel need to know what they have to do to be considered for a promotion to a sales manager.

Training is a huge part of having a career. There should be leadership and management courses available for salespeople interested in sales management. Same goes for F&I courses. Not all courses need to be taught in-house. Your state dealer association offers many valuable courses. So does NADA.

Here is a side note to illustrate that most car dealers do not value training. The Greater New York Dealer Association had a class scheduled to train service advisors how to sell to customers while in the service area. This is a great topic, and majority of dealerships would benefit from it. There are more than 400 dealerships that are members of GNYADA. On average, they employ three service advisors each. So the total pool is 1,200 service advisors, not counting service managers. Unfortunately the class was cancelled because only three people registered. One of them was me.

To summarize, employee training is a costly undertaking but is much more expensive to ignore it.

Rewarding employees helps them feel appreciated. A lot of dealer principals and general managers make a mistake and focus exclusively on financial rewards. Due to changes in parenting and schooling, we are witnessing a generational shift in values. Millennials are not motivated by money as much as Generation X and Baby Boomers. They respond much better to experiences. So, make sure to incorporate experiences into your repertoire. For example, instead of giving a $3,000 bonus to the salesperson who sold the most cars in a calendar year, send him or her and significant other on trip to the Caribbean. Trust me, the salesperson will love it.

Company dinners and Christmas parties are a phenomenal morale-building exercises. Celebrate with your team every time, they hit a milestone. If you finished number one in the zone or if you achieved a certain customer satisfaction score, make sure to celebrate. Also, have a salesperson of the month board. Let's not forget service here. Create a service advisor of the month and a technician of the month board.

To complete the process, have an employee of the month board and develop a criteria that covers all employees. It is not always about car sales or hours per repair order. Customer service, referral business and internal cooperation should count, too.

According to studies, employees are not as motivated by profits as they are of finding meaning in their work. They want to feel they are not just working but having a positive impact. When your employees feel that way, you will have a great team.

8
ORGANIZATIONAL MISSION STATEMENT

IF YOUR DEALERSHIP doesn't have a mission statement or a goal, it will be really hard to formulate a strategy. A mission statement serves as the guiding light for all of your decisions. A good mission statement is concise and easily understood while providing an overview of the dealership's goals. It should reflect the values that you aspire to and present the vision you have for the dealership.

If I were to go back to retail, this would be my mission statement:

To provide the most transparent and customer-centric buying experience and the most expert service/repair experience as well as the most comprehensive selection of parts.

This particular mission statement forces all departments to work together in order to satisfy consumers' needs.

Transparency calls for clear pricing on new and used cars, and trade-ins on and off line, and digital retail. A customer-centric buying experience and expert service requires ongoing training for sales and service departments. Comprehensive selection of parts calls for working with retail and wholesale customers and not conceding market share to aftermarket parts providers.

The key here is to make sure that employees and customers know your mission statement. To accomplish that, you will need to put it up in your showroom and website. In addition, mission statement needs to be reinforced through regular employee training/meetings.

It is considered the best practice to display a code of ethics on the dealership's website and in the showroom/customer waiting area. As you know, car dealers do not have a good reputation. Displaying code of ethics on the website and incorporating it into the walk around could help reduce customers' apprehension.

No need to reinvent the wheel here. You can use the code of ethics developed by NADA:

- Operate this business in accord with the highest standards of ethical conduct.

- Treat each customer in a fair, open, and honest manner, and fully comply with all laws that prohibit discrimination.

- Meet the transportation needs of our customers in a knowledgeable and professional manner.

- Represent our products clearly and factually, standing fully behind our warranties, direct and implied, and in all other ways justifying the customer's respect and confidence.

- Advertise our products in a positive, factual, and informative manner.

- Detail charges to assist our customers in understanding repair work and provide written estimates of any service work to be performed, upon request, or as required by law.

- Resolve customer concerns promptly and courteously.
- Put our promises in writing and stand behind them.

It's not enough to post the signs; you have to live up to the words.

9
BUILDING THE TEAM

THE ONLY WAY to build an effective team is to have a compelling vision for the business and offer employees a career, not a job. One of the most important ingredients of a great team is talent. Building a talented team is what separates professional leaders from competition.

There are two aspects that are worth discussing: attracting and then retaining talent.

Let's start with attracting quality employees.

There are reasons why dealership do not attract high-level employees, including the bad reputation of automotive retail, long hours, and no educational requirements. We need to change peoples' perception of our business if we want to survive.

Dealer principals and general managers must actively participate in high school and college job fairs and career days. They need to make a compelling case why it is a good choice to work in a car dealership. There needs to be a summer internship program that introduces students to various roles in a car dealership. Automotive retail is a sophisticated business that can offer a career in many fields, including sales, management, accounting, customer service, marketing, advertising and inventory management.

Selling cars is the engine that allows for additional revenue sources. That's why everybody should spend a certain time in sales in order to fully appreciate the business. For example, at Enterprise, everybody starts as a rental agent. At Zappos, everybody starts in customer service.

There is a need for a full-time human resources (HR) manager because you cannot expect that job candidates will just appear from thin air. HR manager has to coordinate with local high schools and colleges, create compelling help-wanted ads, develop attractive pay plans, benefits, and perks. This is what it takes to attract quality personnel in the environment of full employment.

Here are suggestions for attracting top employees:

1. **Expand Search**

    Make sure jobs are listed on all appropriate websites with an overview of the dealership culture, clear job description and explanation of career paths and benefits. In essence, you are making a position with a dealership as promising and rewarding as a position in any company.

2. **Provide Perks**

    Quality applicants have many options. You can attract your share by offering special benefits, such as help to pay college tuition, training and other benefits. Other companies do that now; you will have to match them.

Now, how can you retain these quality employees?

We all know that employee turnover is expensive, so we have to do whatever it takes to retain good people. Below are some ideas that should help you:

1. Healthy work environment
2. Clean and modern facility
3. Reasonable schedule

4. Fair pay
5. Career growth through training.

In addition, it makes no sense to hire talented people and not provide them with the necessary training to be successful. Make sure you work closely with your HR department to develop a comprehensive cultural immersion program. After all, onboarding of new hires and ongoing training of existing employees are among the main functions of the HR manager.

Finding and retaining quality employees is the basis of a dealership's success. Payroll often exceeds 50 percent of a dealership budget. You can't afford high turnover, weak onboarding or poor hiring practices.

10
DEFINING CUSTOMER EXPERIENCE (WALK-IN)

CUSTOMERS GO INTO showrooms. They just don't enjoy the experience. In a recent study, car dealerships fared very poorly: 87 percent of Americans dislike something about car shopping at dealerships; 61 percent feel they're taken advantage of while there. According to the research, 52 percent of car shoppers "feel anxious or uncomfortable at dealerships." The younger generation say they'd rather clean their homes or wait in line at DMV. About 24 percent said they would prefer to get a root canal.

That's not very encouraging.

Invariably, car shoppers make it clear that they prefer to buy from someone they have dealt with before. Other positives include: referral from a trust friend and a good salesperson. That's why you need top-notch employees.

Often, because a vast majority of dealer principals and general managers have sales background, they focus on the customer experience in the sales and F&I departments. That's too narrow.

A better approach would be to look at all aspects of the customer experience: sales, BDC, F&I, service, parts, digital, etc.

Let's start with the in-showroom customer experience. We are going to begin with an easy and increasingly rare situation: a walk-in customer with no appointment. The key is to have a systematic approach to ensure that all customers are handled the same way.

1. Based on the physical layout of the showroom, does the customer see the receptionist first? If so, is there a well-defined protocol of assigning a customer to a salesperson?
2. Is there a systematic approach to selling cars or each salesperson has his or her own unique way?
3. Are there well-defined steps to the sale that each salesperson follows?
4. Does the salesperson enter the customer into the Customer Relationship Management (CRM) in real time?
5. Is the customer taken on a test drive?
6. Are cars readily available for a test drive?
7. Is there a defined test drive route?
8. Is the trade-in appraised?
9. How long does the appraisal take?
10. Is the customer taking an active part in the appraisal process?
11. Is there a firm offer to buy a customer's vehicle even if he doesn't buy a car?
12. How long does it take to make a deal?
13. Does the sales manager introduce himself?

14. How long before the customer sees a finance manager?
15. Is there an interview conducted by the F&I manager?
16. Does the salesperson or delivery coordinator go over the car before or after F&I?
17. How long is the F&I process?
18. Is a menu being used during F&I?
19. Are all products presented and explained?
20. Is there an introduction to the service department?
21. Is the customer enrolled into a loyalty program?
22. Is the customer offered an encore delivery?
23. Does the dealership have an app and is the customer asked to download it?
24. Is the customer-referral program reviewed at the time of delivery?
25. Is the customer told about additional related businesses, such as a body shop, car rental, etc.?
26. What is the follow-up process after the purchase?

Answering these questions will help you create a well-defined sales process.

The next step is to train everybody involved in the process. A lot of general managers make a mistake focusing all their energy on training the sales staff. You need to make sure to involve everyone in the dealership in training, including parking valet, receptionist, salespeople, sales managers, F&I managers and delivery coordinators.

Then, all employees should practice/rehearse and stress test the process in order to perfect it. Training must be ongoing and often repetitive.

You want to understand what may concern a customer. You can find out through consumer surveys and on-line reviews. Be sure to pick up threads that may mention your dealership. Most people only mention problems. Once you can identify those sore points, do what you can to eliminate them.

11
DEFINING CUSTOMER EXPERIENCE (BDC)

UNFORTUNATELY, THE DAYS of walk-in traffic are long gone. Majority of customers start the buying process online by first researching the car and then researching the dealership where they will end up buying it. After narrowing down the vehicle and the dealership online reputation, including ease of use of dealership's website, among other issues, the customer will either call or email.

This initial contact has tremendous implications. If your Business Development Center 9CRM) is a well-oiled machine, then the probability of the customer making appointment and showing up is much greater. Again, we have to realize that a lot of dealer principals and general manager came up through the ranks before BDC department was a true necessity. This is why a lot of them don't place a lot of emphasis on it.

Here is the easiest way to prove this point. Do you know that the average salary of a BDC manager is $36,000 a year? Let's assume for a second that this statistic is wrong and the true number is $72,000. Do you honestly think that you can get a superstar performer to run this mission-critical department for $72,000? I really doubt it considering that this person can make double as a sales manager or triple as finance manager.

Let's start with a list of items that should help you define and measure customer experience with the BDC department:

1. If a live receptionist answers the phone, how long is the transfer to BDC?
2. Is the transfer to BDC or to an available salesperson?
3. Is there a detailed script that staff has to adhere to?
4. Do staffers disclose sales price/lease price on the phone? If they don't, it will be really hard for your dealership to survive in the age of transparency and convenience.
5. Is every incoming sales call entered into the CRM?
6. Are email addresses being collected during the call?
7. Is there a follow-up email being sent to the customer?
8. Is appointment confirmation being sent to the customer?
9. Are templates being used?
10. Do employees understand email etiquette?
11. Are appointments being confirmed?
12. Does the BDC staff have the necessary product knowledge?
13. How long is an average call?
14. Does BDC staff ask for an appointment?
15. If customer makes an appointment for a test drive, how is this information communicated to the sales department?
16. Who is responsible for the car being ready for test drive?

17. Does BDC staff have access to Dealership Management Software (DMS) to desk a deal?

It is your job to make sure that your BDC department is doing its job. We all know the saying that you can't manage it if you can't measure it. We need to understand what we are looking at in order to improve it:

1. What is the pay plan of BDC staff? Remember that pay plans drive behavior, and you might want to incentivize shows and sold customers.
2. What type of a script is being used? Did you write it? Do you use a BDC training company?
3. What Key Performance Indicators (KPI) do you measure? Average length of calls, number of outbound calls, appointment ratio, show ration, etc.?
4. Is CRM being used religiously?
5. How often do you find yourself spending time in BDC?
6. Do you listen to incoming calls?
7. Does the BDC manager listen to the incoming calls?
8. How often do you review incoming calls and train?

Most of all, sales staff have to be personable. About 86 percent of consumers said personalization had some effect on their buying decisions.

12
DEFINING CUSTOMER EXPERIENCE (SERVICE)

SERVICE DEPARTMENT WILL make or break your dealership. Good service department will produce repeat and referral business, feed your sales department and vice versa. Understanding and improving service department will separate you from competition and help you survive the next sales downturn.

I would encourage every dealer principal and general manager to spend a lot of time in service. I would even go as far as relocating your office to service. Service enjoys extremely high profit margins, and majority of customers do not even consider negotiating.

There are three reasons people come to service:

1. Scheduled maintenance

2. Repair

3. Recall.

According to a 2018 Cox Automotive study, about 70 percent of your car-purchasing customers won't return for service. That works out to about $15.9 million in lost revenue per franchise dealership.

The same study found that service consumers are motivated by two things:

1. Convenience
2. Lack of stress.

You can offer that by adopting several conveniences:

1. On-line billpaying
2. On-line bill payment with mobile devices
3. Easy scheduling
4. Videos of recommended service
5. Estimates provided on-line with the ability to approve or disapprove
6. Guaranteed loaners
7. Frequent updates

Other suggestions based on data include:

8. Offer a warm, welcoming service
9. Demonstrate competence with videos and explanations
10. Provide benefits, such as free oil changes
11. Use transparent pricing. In surveys, customers say value is more important that even quality, convenience or trust.

13
DEFINING CUSTOMER SERVICE (EXPRESS SERVICE)

I DON'T THINK customers want to make appointments for scheduled maintenance because they know that there is no appointment necessary at Jiffy Lube or any other independent mechanic. If you still require an appointment for an oil change, then you are completely missing the point. It is a good idea to have an express service with a dedicated service advisor in order to compete with independents. Make sure that you perform an oil change in a timely manner. Otherwise, your customers will not be coming back.

The best practice is to have an A-tech oversee the work of lube technicians in order to increase upsell of repair work. In addition, make sure to measure the following KPIs:

1. How long it takes to change oil? You might have to sit there with a stopwatch.

2. Upsell percentage of filters, tire rotation, bulbs, etc. These percentages must be tracked on a daily/weekly/monthly basis.

3. Overall wait time from pulling in to pulling out. Thirty minutes or less is the magic number.

Promoting express service must be a part of the advertising budget. Promote it in several ways:

1. Dealership website
2. Signage in the showroom and service waiting area
3. Google pay per click
4. Email campaigns
5. Direct mail.

It is also a good idea to have your BDC department conduct an outbound phone campaign. BDC should reach out to all customers who, based on your records, are due for an oil change and let them know that your prices are competitive and that you do not require an appointment. At this point, you should have customer-convenient business hours, for example, 7am to midnight.

You have to offer Express Service for all makes and models if you are serious about competing with Jiffy Lube and similar companies. Your parts department should have oil filters, cabin filters, etc. for most popular cars in your market.

Here are some things to consider with express service:

1. Should you affiliate with an automaker's quick-service program or design your own?
2. Operate quick service in a separate building or integrate into the main shop?

3. If the operation is separate, is it on or off the dealership site?

4. Do you offer customers a time guarantee for completion?

5. Do you advertise the price?

6. Do you require appointments or take all comers?

7. Do you offer quick service during evenings and on weekends?

8. Do you accept other brands of vehicles?

9. Did you decide which maintenance and repair work should be included in express service?

Prices should be competitive. However, consumers repeatedly value time over price. An efficient, friendly visit to your service department outweighs other factors.

14
DEFINING CUSTOMER EXPERIENCE WITH REPAIRS AND RECALLS

REPAIRS ARE DIFFERENT from oil changes and scheduled maintenance. Pay special attention to repair work for vehicles not covered by a factory warranty. This is by far the most profitable customer-paid labor. Often, independent mechanics do not have the necessary expertise and special tools to do certain repairs. As a result, at this point, you are only competing with local franchise dealers.

You need to make sure that the entire process makes sense from the customer perspective. Customers have to be able to either make an appointment online or by phone. You should use shop-loading software to ensure the best customer experience.

Let's quickly talk about appointments. Do not overbook because this is the easiest way to disappoint your customers and really defeats the whole purpose of an appointment. For example, an 11am appointment means that the customer will pull into the service drive and meet the service advisor around 11. If the customer pulls in on time and has to wait for 10 or 20 minutes for an advisor, it is very unlikely that the customer will be back. At this point, your dealership will have lost all future service and parts revenue as well as a chance to sell a new or used car. In addition, customer might leave a bad review online and deter more customers from visiting your service department.

Once you quantify this financial loss, you will be all over service department.

Should you offer vehicle pick-up and drop-off? I think it is a great idea. Since customers often do not have to wait and interrupt their day, they are more likely to agree to recommended work. Your dollars per repair order will be going up along with customer satisfaction.

Should you offer loaners, shuttle customers, or use Uber or Lyft? This is a tough decision because many car dealers I work with are under constant pressure from OEMs to put new cars in their loaner fleet. Since both OEMs and dealers are addicted to volume, they can hit their numbers by putting new cars into loaner service.

Loaner vehicles are not real retail sales and only mislead shareholders. In addition, there are many costs associated with running a loaner fleet, including gas, tolls, and tickets. Providing shuttle service might be expensive (cost of shuttle, gas, tolls, driver salary, insurance) and inefficient. Using Lyft or Uber seems to be the most economical approach as long as you put some limitations on it.

Communicating with customers about the status of the repair or recall is critical to the success of your service department. If the customer has to call you to find out about his or her car, you failed and most likely will never see this customer again. It is the service advisor's responsibility to stay in touch with the customer. Make sure you know the customer's cell phone number and email address. Recommended service work should be communicated electronically and give a customer the ability to authorize or decline it via a cell phone or computer. Video is especially effective.

Active delivery is the best practice. A service advisor should actively do a quick walkaround and explain what was done and that everything is all right. It is a good idea to schedule declined work for the next visit immediately. If you offer vehicle pick-up and drop-off, then an active walkaround should be done electronically.

I can't stress enough that customers love to pick up a clean car. Offering free car wash with every service is a great investment and will pay for itself through customer retention and satisfaction.

15
ROLE OF BDC IN DEFINING CUSTOMER EXPERIENCE IN SERVICE

NOW LET'S TALK about the role of BDC and how it affects customer experience and shop-loading. Service BDC is there to make appointments and to conduct outgoing campaigns for recalls and declined work. There should be a process to identify sold vehicles with open recalls and contact these customers as long as parts are in stock. Service and Parts managers should work closely with the BDC department in order to identify these vehicles.

Service advisors absolutely must record declined work on the repair order. There has to be an op code for declined work. This way, your service manager can run a report and have BDC department contact these customers to schedule declined work for their next visit.

Another best practice is to send out an email survey to each service customer. Design a short survey that customers can answer in less than a minute and make continuous improvements to your process based on the results. Here are some sample questions:

1. Did you see the service advisor at the scheduled time?
2. Did service advisor go over your car in the service drive?
3. Did service advisor communicate with you about the status of your car?
4. Was the issue fixed?
5. Was the vehicle returned clean?

16
DEFINING CUSTOMER EXPERIENCE IN PARTS (1)

A PARTS DEPARTMENT located facing customers enjoys a captive audience of clients waiting for their cars. The idea here is to have a well-organized retail shop with a variety of parts and accessories on display. The problem is that you are limited to the customers waiting in your service department.

The internet has trained all of us to shop online. So, the best thing you can do to learn digital retail is to start selling parts online. Selling online means you are no longer limited to waiting and local customers. People from all over the world could be your potential customers. I work with car dealers that sell about 3 percent of their parts to international customers. It is not unheard of for them to sell a set of floor mats to a customer in Italy.

There are two ways to do it: directly from your dealership's website or by building a dedicated website. Either way is fine. The key is to have a complete parts catalog online with a simple shipping calculator and checkout process. Then, you have to allocate advertising dollars to promote it.

Here is my personal experience buying floor mats for my new car. I will not name names, but here is what happened. I live in New York City and bought a new car at a local dealer. I quickly realized that I need all-weather mats and did a quick Google search. To my surprise not one local dealer showed up on the first page of Google.

Then I visited three local dealerships' websites and tried to find these floor mats but couldn't. I then called two dealerships and was told that these floor mats are in stock and that the price is $199; however, they didn't even try to sell me over the phone. I ended up buying these floor mats from a dealership in Massachusetts for $119.

This is a clear illustration of one dealership understanding the beauty of e-commerce. The Massachusetts dealership didn't have as much local business but found a way to sell products at a distance.

You shouldn't even think about selling cars online unless you can first figure out parts sales.

17
DEFINING CUSTOMER EXPERIENCE IN PARTS (2)

WHETHER YOU LIKE or not Amazon is the leader in e-commerce and logistics. Amazon is the ultimate everything store, and more and more people shop there every day. If your dealership is not offering parts for sale on Amazon, you are missing a huge opportunity.

It takes effort and hard work to understand the way Amazon fulfillment centers operate. Once you master it, you will be in a position to exponentially expand your market.

Keep in mind that selling parts on Amazon is different than selling parts wholesale. Profit margins on Amazon sales are much higher because people are willing to pay more – especially Prime customers – for convenience, transparency, quick shipping and easy returns.

Do not forget that Walmart is doing whatever it can to catch up with Amazon. It is a good idea to become a seller on Walmart's website along with any other sites potential customers logically might search, such as eBay. In that way, your dealership can offer multiple options for parts customers.

In order for this approach to succeed, you will have to appoint a dedicated person whose sole responsibility is selling parts online. This person has to become your liaison to all vendors, understand shipping and returns, and communicate with customers. With time, you will have to add more people to this department because an increasing number of consumers prefer e-commerce.

18
ADDITIONAL PROFIT CENTERS

NEW CAR MARGINS are almost non-existent, used cars are getting harder to make money on, and there is pressure from online retailers as well as from independent mechanics. As the general manager, your main priority is to run a profitable business. The more profit centers you develop, the easier it is going to survive cyclical car business. Every so many years, there is a sales downturn.

With high service retention, you can offset losses in the sales department. As cars become more sophisticated and use better lubricants, the frequency of service visits will diminish. To offset losses in service revenue, your dealership must develop additional profit centers.

One of the most obvious involves following up on leads. There are several steps to take that can improve sales:

1. **Quick response**

    Any lead should be followed up within five minutes via phone call, email, text message or other route. If the salesperson doesn't reach the potential customer on the first try, he or she should try again. Be careful not to flood voicemail or email addresses. Customers resent that.

Also, be sure that the salesperson has all the information about the lead before the contact is made. Computers record where customers went on your site so the salesperson can narrow down what the customer is looking for. That way, no one wastes time.

2. **Personal**

    All initial contact should involve an individual, not automation. A human touch works far better, and salespersons can supply answers that an automated system may not be able to. Of course, in a few years, artificial intelligence may make us all irrelevant. In the interim, have a person call.

3. **Follow procedure**

    Leads may be pre-qualified, but the sales staff needs to follow your dealership's normal procedure to complete the sale.

4. **Provide a perk**

    Offer something of value to any customer who uses your website. That can range from a coupon for some service, a promotion just for on-line customers or special financing. Be creative.

Outside of sales, however, dealerships can still find avenues to more revenue. We already discussed two options in the previous chapters:

1. Express Service

2. Selling parts online

Other possibilities to boost revenue are listed below. We will look at each one in turn.

1. Tire Sales
2. Detail center
3. Customization
4. F&I products online
5. Wholesale
6. Commercial accounts. Actively go after Uber/Lyft, taxi fleets to ensure that you working towards 100-percent shop utilization.
7. Dealer-owned prepaid maintenance\post-sale F&I product follow-up
8. Dealer-owned subscriptions
9. Dealer-owned insurance
10. Body shop

19
TIRE SALES

MAJORITY OF CAR owners do not buy tires from new car dealerships. As a matter of fact, more than 90 percent of tires are bought in one of the following places:

1. Branded tire chains (Firestone, Goodyear)
2. Big box retailer (Walmart)
3. Online retailer (TireRack.com)
4. Tire retail chain (Tire Kingdom)
5. Independent mechanic/tire shop

Car dealers get about 8.5 percent of the business.

Nevertheless, there is a significant revenue opportunity in tire sales. In order to achieve it, you will need to re-evaluate your marketing, merchandising, service advising and customer education, and service-drive processes.

First, let's start with an easy one: marketing. Do not expect a lot of tire sales, if you keep it a secret. Have a page on your website dedicated to tires. In all of your service marketing campaigns, mention that you carry tires. Spend money on pay-per-click advertising. Remember that the main reason car dealers do not sell enough tires is because they don't tell customers that they are in the tire business.

Merchandising is a science that big retailers have mastered. Car dealers, on the other hand, are really behind when it comes to even appreciating merchandising in service. Most car dealers apparently employ an out-of-sight out-of-mind merchandising strategy.

Without a tire display in the service drive, you will have trouble selling tires. Best practice is offer Good-Better-Best tire displays. In addition, do not forget to have signage in the customer-waiting area. Another best practice is to have service advisors wear an "Ask Me About Tires" pin.

Dealers have to educate advisors and customers about tires. This is not easy. People are creatures of habit, and service advisors are no different. Is there a way to change habits or form new ones? The answer is yes. There are only two reasons why service staffers are not selling tires:

1. Nobody told them to do it.

2. They do not know how.

3. They are not incentivized to do it.

Someone – dealer principal, general manager, service manager – at the dealership must make tire sales a priority and offer incentives to service advisors. Do not forget that pay plans drive behavior.

Once tires are purchased, tire displays installed, and pay plans modified, you will need to invest into training. Your service advisors must understand why and how to sell tires. They must be knowledgeable about tires. They should be able to use simple word tracks when interacting with customers.

Moreover, it is a good idea to promote a price-match guarantee and offer tire replacement and protection plans similar to those offered by aftermarket retailers. Service advisors must be able to show the value of buying from the dealership.

Technology can be very helpful when it comes to tire sales. You could install a wheel alignment machine that also has a tire thread measure function. It literally takes seconds to determine if the vehicle needs new tires and/or alignment. Customers see color-coded results either on a big screen TV or via a computer printout.

Consider other possibilities, such as offering free rotations or inspections to new customers. You also can host tire safety seminars for teenagers and their parents. These programs can help build awareness of your tire business and loyalty.

Inventory should not be a major problem. As a dealer, you only need to carry tires for cars you sell. Research your market to determine the types of tires needed in your area and be sure to have them in stock.

Finally, you won't sell anything if you don't ask. Service advisors must be trained to ask for the order. It is your responsibility to monitor tire sales penetration and to hold advisors accountable.

20
DETAIL CENTER

FIRST IMPRESSIONS MATTER. When customers come to your used car lot, you must have cars there in pristine condition. If you don't, it will take you longer to turn inventory, increasing your floor-plan expense. One way or another, you will need get your inventory frontline ready. That requires detailing.

There are two ways to detail: outsource or do in-house.

If you decide to outsource, then consider the following:

1. Quality of work

2. Price

3. Turnaround time/capacity

4. Insurance

Doing it in-house gives you complete control of the operation and allows you to also offer detailing services to retail customers. That leads to an additional revenue stream.

In order to have a successful detailing operation, you will need to understand the business, including what it means to detail a car and how long it takes, what equipment and chemicals to buy as well as EPA and OSHA rules. In addition, you will need to find and train good people.

I personally like to be in control of my destiny and feel that car dealers should have an in-house detail operation. Remember that there is a dual benefit: Getting your inventory frontline ready and generating additional revenue.

The extra money will only come if you make an investment in training service advisors, add detail to the service menu, and invest in signage and advertising.

Final thought on detailing: Detailers cannot be left to their own devices. Someone needs to be in charge and manage the operation. You don't have to hire a dedicated manager in the beginning. Consider adding more responsibilities to your service manager.

21
CUSTOMIZATION

WE ALL HAVE our individual styles. People express themselves through clothes, hairstyle, make-up, etc. Many owners think the same way about their cars. In many cases, vehicle serve as the ultimate expression of one's lifestyle. Choosing a particular car to drive is the foundation of that expression. For example, driving a Toyota 4Runner might emphasize the love of outdoors and the spirit of exploration while driving a Ford Mustang could reflect a love of freedom and speed.

Many vehicle owners want to take this expression of individualism to the next level via accessories. Selling accessories is another revenue stream that, unfortunately, many car dealers neglect.

According to *Automotive News*, about 7 million vehicles sold annually are accessorized within the first two years of ownership. Average spend is $1,950 per car. This a huge market to take advantage of.

The first step is to accessorize vehicles in the showroom prior to the sale. This approach helps build a dealership's identity, stand out from competition and get away from competing on price. Accessorizing vehicles in the showroom puts the emphasis on accessories and starts a much-needed conversation with customers. Skipping this step is just another way of saying "out of sight, out of mind."

Remember, pay plans drive behavior. As with so much of sales success, your accessory sales will start happening if you offer incentives to your sales staff.

The next step is to display accessories not just in the showroom but in your retail store and customer-waiting area, and on your website. It is important to display prices that include installation. Again, with proper marketing and merchandising, you can enjoy a healthy revenue stream/profit center.

22
SELLING F&I PRODUCTS ONLINE

F&I PRODUCTS – such as GAP, vehicle service contracts, tires and wheels, interior and exterior protection, key replacements –have been around for a long time and help customers deal with unpredictable circumstances in a financially manageable way. It is better to purchase GAP protection for $700 than to deal with a $5,000 GAP in case of a total loss.

Unfortunately, most dealer principals and general managers feel that F&I is their only remaining profit center since margins are virtually nonexistent on new car sales. They are afraid to display F&I products online and still rely on high-pressure sales tactics in the F&I office.

Meanwhile consumers are moving in a totally different direction. They are used to doing research and having all the necessary information at their fingertips. This is exactly why car dealers need to display F&I products, explain their features and benefits. This approach will only help increase product penetration. In addition, there should be a way for consumers to buy these F&I

products right from the dealership's website. Technology is out there to do just that.

Here is the tricky part: if you display F&I products and offer them for sale on your website, there has to be price consistency between online sales and showroom sales. You must sell these products for the same price.

23
WHOLESALE

WHOLESALE USED TO be simple. Some guy would come once a week and buy your trades. These days are long gone, and you might want to approach it differently in order to make additional profit.

First, you can take your wholesale units to the auction yourself. I know many large auto groups that do exactly that. This way they don't leave any money on the table.

Second, you can and should list your wholesale units on the auction's website. This approach will increase the turn time.

Other tips include:

1. Think of it as you would retail. The more information, the better. Use photos, video and selling points as you would with a new car.

2. Post information to on-line sites and avoid the expense of shipping cars to an auction house.

3. If a used car has sat on your lot for 45 days, post it on an on-line auction site to increase visibility.

4. Price the car to get rid of it. A used car no one wants is simply dead money.

When we talk about wholesale, most car dealers think of wholesaling their undesirable trade-ins or old units. There is a flipside to wholesale – buying cars.

It is always cheaper to buy cars directly from customers compared to the auction. At the very minimum, you are saving on the auction fee and transportation.

To do that, you must develop a strategy to acquire inventory directly from consumers. Consider providing a firm offer for the trade-in even if the customer decides not to buy a new car from you. Promote this service on your website and in your marketing. Place signs in in the showroom and in the service department as well.

24
SERVICING FLEET ACCOUNTS

INSTEAD OF WORRYING about how rideshare companies are going to revolutionize the way we get from point A to point B and change the way consumers buy cars, let's examine a clear opportunity to make money instead.

There are hundreds of thousands cars that are used in the ride-sharing business. For example, in New York City alone, Uber/Lyft/Juno/Via use a combined about 100,000 vehicles. These cars are being used day and night and require maintenance at much shorter intervals compared to regular passenger vehicles.

Your service manager should proactively reach out to all the rideshare fleet operators as well as individual drivers. Keep in mind that all the maintenance work will lead to profitable customer-pay labor repair work. Fleet owners and individual owner operators cannot afford not to do the work because they need these cars running.

Besides rideshare vehicles, there are plenty of corporate fleets and city/state governments cars to service. All you have to do is actively reach out to them and make a compelling case why your service department is best suited to handle the work.

Just imagine opening an extra shift. I promise the extra labor and parts sales will make a huge difference in your service absorption and shop utilization.

Besides, all these drivers and corporations will consider your dealership when it comes to upgrading their fleets.

25
DEALER-OWNED PREPAID MAINTENANCE

CAR BUSINESS IS not that different from other business. The main idea is to sell a car and then retain the customer in service. This approach allows you to increase earnings per lifetime of a customer. So, service retention is key to additional service and parts profit as well as to additional car sales.

Unfortunately, service retention among new car dealership is pretty low. No more than 30 percent of customers perform scheduled maintenance at a selling dealership. Obviously, that means 70 percent of customers go elsewhere.

Implementing dealer-owned prepaid maintenance at your dealership is a must. Here is how it works.

When you choose to sell an OEM prepaid maintenance, you are giving a license to your customers to go to any of your competitors to do the work. For example, if you sell Honda prepaid maintenance, your customers can go to any Honda dealership. Instead, consider Dealer-Owned Prepaid Maintenance that is only good at your service department.

The best approach is to give away the first year of prepaid maintenance and upsell to three- or five-year plans in F&I. Giving away the first year of prepaid maintenance helps enhance your "why buy from us" story and stand out from competition.

Dealer-Owned Prepaid Maintenance is administered by a third party that provides marketing materials, training, web portal for tracking, and ultimately contacts customers numerous times to drive them to your service department. Utilizing this approach will increase service retention to 70-75 percent. The good news is that 20-25 percent of customers pay premiums and then do not show up. That's pure profit.

With this approach, your customers get used to coming to your service department while your service advisors are in a position to build relationships. These relationships will count when the time comes to upsell additional work.

There are other plusses:

Positive

1. Many plans offer incentives to salesmen.

2. The policy guarantees your mechanics will be busy. That leads not only to repeat business but the likelihood a service customer will buy a new car from you.

3. Customers appreciate knowing that their costs are fixed and spread across the life of the policy. They don't have to think about maintenance costs anymore. At the same time, you maintain contact with the customer to remind about needed service. That builds relationships, the lifeblood of a good business.

26
POST-SALE F&I PRODUCT FOLLOW-UP

LET'S BE HONEST: at most dealerships, there is no F&I follow-up. If a customer says no to the purchase of F&I products, that customer is completely forgotten. F&I managers do not have the desire or the time to follow up, and BDC department doesn't have the expertise to do it.

That represents a missed opportunity. In many cases, customers walk into the F&I office with their guard up and say 'no" to everything being presented. There is a lot of negative information regarding F&I products on the web, an issue that really needs to be addressed by the F&I product providers.

Rather than forget the customers, your F&I manager could set up a follow-up process with these customers in a week or two weeks after delivery. They are no longer in the dealership and feel relaxed. They have also taken possession of the car and have a pride of ownership. At this point, they might be much more receptive to buying a vehicle service contract or tire and wheel protection.

There is technology available to do this follow-up electronically. Basically, an email goes out with all declined products and a discount coupon. Customer clicks on the link, and there is a digital checkout. Copies of the contracts are automatically emailed to the customer. This is a really good approach since the dealership doesn't have to pay F&I commissions.

I believe that car business is still a relationship business and having technology is great but it is not as effective without a human touch. This is why I strongly believe this follow-up should be done by the finance managers. They should have the necessary product knowledge and social skills to get this done.

As incentive, post-sale F&I follow-up and penetration must be part of their compensation.

In addition, finance managers must have the time to do it. To succeed, you must make sure the department is properly staffed. The industry is standard is no more than 80 deals per month per finance manager. In my opinion, you can bring it down to 65 deals and free them up for the post-sale follow-up.

Another approach is to train your BDC reps and pay them a commission on each sale. This is not as easy as it sounds because you would need to train them on all F&I products.

Ultimately, it does not matter whether you choose to go with an electronic solution or a people solution or a combination of both. What really matters is that you actually do it.

27
DEALER-OWNED SUBSCRIPTIONS

THE IDEA BEHIND subscriptions is relatively simple. A customer pays a set monthly fee and then can change cars several times a month. OEMs like Cadillac and BMW pioneered the concept. So far, few car dealers have jumped onboard. A recent survey found only 4 percent of dealers offer this amenity. Fully 33 percent of dealers never heard of it.

That's likely to change. I don't think that subscriptions are going to replace the way people buy or lease cars, but a percentage of population is interested in it. Projections show the car subscriptions market growing by 71 percent by 2022.

If you follow me on social media, you know that I am very vocal when it comes to OEM subscriptions. My view is simple: OEM subscription is a clear violation of franchise laws. Car dealers must oppose it through their state dealer associations as well via the National Automobile Dealer Association. Franchise laws were written to prevent the automakers from selling or leasing cars directly to consumers. At that time, there was no concept of subscriptions, so they are not clearly prohibited by these laws.

OEM subscriptions are problematic because if you are, for example, a Volvo dealer, you are now competing with your own factory for the same customer. This is the factory that makes you spend millions of dollars on facility upgrades and might withhold allocation to promote their subscription model.

Besides, in my view, car dealers are much better positioned to offer subscriptions than any OEM. Here is why:

First, car dealers can offer a subscription that includes different makes. Remember that OEM subscription is just one make. Volvo subscription means that the customer can only drive different models of Volvo. If you look at it from the consumer perspective, it is much more fun to switch from one make to another. For example, I would love to go from a Ford 150 to Dodge Challenger to Mercedes Benz E Class.

Second, software that OEMs use to run their subscriptions is available to car dealers. The name of the software provider is Clutch, whose software helps you manage your fleet so you know when to take the customer out of a particular car.

Third, subscription basically means one, all-inclusive, monthly payment covering car payment. car insurance and maintenance. Vehicles in the dealership's subscription fleet must be maintained at the dealership's service department and that keeps your technicians busy.

Fourth, you don't have to put new cars into the subscription model. Off-lease vehicles are great, and they already have taken a depreciation hit.

On the negative side, dealers who have started a subscription program say the expense can run up to $500,000 to start.

However, benefits seem to outweigh costs. Dealers report now they are averaging about $200 a car profit with subscription customers. In addition, dealers see customers far more often, building those all-important relationships.

It's clear that car dealers are much better suited to provide subscriptions to their customers. Give it a shot, and don't let OEMs take what is rightfully yours.

28
DEALER-OWNED INSURANCE AGENCY

IN 2012, ALLSTATE introduced a dealer service program that allowed auto dealers to open Allstate agencies in their showrooms. Since then, other companies have duplicated that approach. However, you can get this done on your own.

It's a natural. Selling cars and auto insurance goes together like peanut butter and jelly. Every customer that buys a car from you buys insurance elsewhere. So, why not start a dealer-owned insurance agency in house?

You have to be willing to invest time and money. First, either you or another designated person must go to school and become a licensed insurance agent. Second, you will have to allocate space and provide all the necessary tools for your agency to succeed – signs, computer, phone, CRM, etc.

Most importantly, you will have to create a process where every customer is provided a quote. Every customer means not just sales customers, but service customers as well. Your service waiters are the perfect candidates to receive an insurance quote.

You see how these numbers can snowball. Furthermore, there is an opportunity to cross-sell home insurance, renters' insurance as well as life insurance and annuities.

The bottom line is that home and life insurance are really sticky. That means consumers rarely shop insurance or switch. So, if your agency is successful, you will be receiving automatic renewal commissions every year for many years to come.

29
DEALER-OWNED BODY SHOP

MAYBE I AM paranoid, but the main reason to have additional sources of income is because car dealers can't rely on just selling cars anymore. Volume is cyclical, and margins are not there.

A body shop is another source of revenue that is worth exploring. Running a body shop is not an easy business. That's why majority of car dealers do not own one. Then again, if it were easy, everybody would do it.

You would need to invest into a new facility, tools and equipment, and hire techs. Then, you have to learn all the intricacies of the business. Start by understanding who your customer is.

At first, you might think that the vehicle owner is the customer. Then, you will realize that the customer's insurance company is the customer, or that the insurance company of another vehicle involved in the accident is the actual customer.

Keeping body work in house has several benefits. First, is providing your retail customers with a full experience in your dealership instead of letting them deal with independents.

Second, and that is especially true for multi-rooftop groups, dealer-owned body shops speed up reconditioning of used cars. We all know that velocity of reconditioning directly affects used car profits. There is a reason why AutoNation and Sonic own body shops.

Third, a body shop provides an opportunity to sell the customer another car. The key is to completely integrate sales and body shop operations.

Fourth, is every dealership has an extensive customer base. Conducting regular marketing campaigns will keep your body shop busy.

Fifth, rideshare vehicles are used much more than regular passenger cars, and the probability of accidents is much higher. Aggressively going after ride-share and taxi body work will keep your techs turning wrenches.

As a final point, diversification is good and will pay off in the long term.

30
MEASURING PERFORMANCE

THERE ARE MANY key performance indicators (KPI) in any business, and car business is no different. Tracking too many KPIs might be overwhelming and, at times, counter-productive. Below, in my opinion, are the most important indicators that every general manager and owner should be tracking:

Sales

- Number of ups on a monthly basis
- Number of incoming phone/internet leads
- Sold customer acquisition cost
- Overall closing ratio
- Average time to complete a deal
- Average age of used car inventory

- Average front-end profit
- Percentage of test-drives
- Average down payment
- Percentage of referrals
- Online reviews
- Average reconditioning time
- Number of unique website visitors
- Sources of web traffic

Service

- Number of repair orders on a monthly basis
- Number of hours sold per repair order
- Effective labor rate
- Number of customers per service advisor
- Percentage of completed multi-point inspections
- Percentage of sold work from multi-point inspections
- Percentage of emails/texts/videos sent out by service advisors recommending additional work
- Percentage of on-line item repair orders
- Service customer acquisition cost

Parts

- Fill rate
- Inventory turns
- Percentage of bins checked on a monthly basis

- Discounting
- Percentage of parts sold online
- Average parts mark-up
- Percentage of pre-paid special order parts
- Lost sales

F&I

- Average back-end profit
- Number of customer per finance manager
- Finance reserve vs. product sales
- Product penetration percentage
- Menu usage
- Time in F&I office
- Product cancellations

HR

- Turnover in the sales department
- Overall turnover
- Percentage of employees trained
- Number of exit interviews conducted

BDC

- Average time to reply to an internet lead
- Average length of incoming sales call
- Appointment show ratio

- Number of all incoming leads
- Number of outgoing calls
- Declined service – number of calls

31
COMMUNICATION

THESE DAYS, MOST communication is done electronically, either through cellphones or computers. That means that the old methods, such as direct mail, are less effective.

Nevertheless, many dealers still continue to send out newsletters, either via the Post Office or email. People just trash that material. There is an alternative – video newsletters.

They are sent via email but contain videos which allow you to chat directly with a customer in an increasingly familiar manner. Studies show that 93 percent of companies worldwide use social media. Your customers are online.

They also don't understand everything they read. Mostly, readers misinterpret the tone of emails. We also aren't very good of conveying tone. That means a lot of writing comes across the wrong way.

Videos solve that problem. With modern technology, they can be produced quickly. They don't have to be long. Just a smiling face and a quick message. No one will misunderstand. People like videos, too. A really good one could even go viral.

Regardless of the choice, good communication both within a dealership and outside is a necessity for success for several reasons:

1. It builds trust. An estimated 71 percent of customers said they bought their new car because they "trusted and respected" their salesperson. Good communication in the dealership creates a trusting atmosphere that translates to the customers.

2. Performance improves when everyone is communicating well. Studies show productivity may jump 20-25 percent in organizations with open communication channels.

3. That, in turn, builds unity. Regular meetings and updates held foster that attitude. Staff then can keep customers informed of anything that will affect them.

4. Good communication also undermines counterproductive gossip and rumors.

32
REVIEWS

ON-LINE REVIEWS ARE quickly becoming a lifeline to customers. People read reviews. They trust reviews far more than celebrity endorsements or anything you say in an ad.

According to research, 72 percent of car buyers will travel 20 to 60 miles extra to visit a dealership that got good reviews. More than 63 percent of people seeking to get their car serviced follow suit. Millennials head the list: an estimated 82 percent of them begin their car-buying adventure by visiting third-party ratings and review sites first

Reviews then are an incredible promotional tool and completely free. However, an estimated 90 percent of customers do not write reviews. Most people don't know where to post one or how.

You can encourage them with an email, thanking the customers for coming to your dealership and including a link to Yelp, TrustPilot, Google + or other site so the customer can easily locate and post a review.

To encourage reviews, you can also offer an incentive, such as a drawing open only to customers who post a review. Even a short note can be helpful. Some dealers have created a Facebook business page to provide a place for a brief review.

You want to be sure to thank anyone who posts a review, good or bad. Besides continuing the relationship, negative reviews will help you weed out a problem.

There won't be too many negative reviews. On average, only about 6 percent of all reviews are negative. That's partially because most reviewers seem to be kind and unwilling to hurt someone's business.

However, if you don't aggressively seek reviews, the percentage of negative reviews can climb to 24 percent. That's because angry people are more motivated to lash out. In response, you need to reach out promptly and offer to work out a solution. That will build your credibility and trust. Do not hesitate to let the public know when you correct a problem. That shows you care about your customers.

33
RELATIONSHIPS

REGARDLESS OF HOW clever you are on line or how many signs you post or how much incentive you offer, your bottom line depends on building relationships.

Customers who have a good experience tell friends.

How can you build solid relationships that can span decades?

For starters, remember that the experience is just as important as the vehicle. Be sure all the information about the vehicles is available via the internet. Be upfront and open. Customers can find out anything to they need to know without ever setting foot in your dealership. If they think you are hiding something or not being aboveboard, they won't stick around.

An estimated 25 percent of car buyers report being unhappy with their dealers. You don't want to be in that group.

Here is some advice:

1. Salespeople need to know their products intimately. Customers expect them to be experts and can be disappointed when not receiving answers.

2. Focus on the customer's needs. Think how you want to be treated if you were buying a car. Treat everyone with courtesy and respect. They are not just customers but a vanguard for their friends and relatives.

3. Provide quality service that meets the highest expectations. Read reviews to catch and eliminate problems.

4. Keep in contact via emails with special offers or just to acknowledge a customer's birthday or anniversary. You don't have to communicate just for sales.

5. Listen to your customers. They will let you know when they are not pleased or even have ideas for improvements. Use every available method of communication. When new technology becomes available, use that, too.

6. Follow through on commitments. Your promises must be kept.

7. Prioritize customers in the dealership. Phone calls can wait. If someone calls while you are with a customer, let your receptionist take a message.

8. Be helpful, even if that means sending a customer somewhere else. The customer will remember and be back.

9. Be sure the forms are completed correctly. No one wants to waste time redoing anything or having to revisit the dealership because of an overlooked item.

10. Keep in contact. Call the customer to see if everything is working out with the car.

Your goal is to make your customer feel welcome and look forward to coming back.

If you succeed, you will have a very successful dealership.

34
CONCLUSION

WE ARE LUCKY because car business is not that complicated, and most of us can execute a plan in order to improve our part of it. Making the plan is easy; execution is the hard part. This book doesn't have any earth-shattering information. In fact, I am sure that you are familiar with many of the concepts discussed here.

The world is changing because of Amazon, Uber and Carvana. Car dealerships are not immune. Amazon, Uber, Carvana are not inventing anything new; they are perfecting an existing process. As a result, transparency and convenience are the pillars of the 21st century e-commerce.

Car dealers have to recognize the threat these companies and changing consumer shopping habits pose to the automotive retail and make the necessary changes before it is too late. No franchise laws are going to save you once Amazon decides to get into this business.

If you really want to compete with Amazon, you have to consider the one-price model. We all know that if Amazon gets into selling cars, it is going to be via the one-price model. CarMax and Carvana are posting sales close to 1 million cars a year to prove that consumers like the one-price model.

The best leaders are always willing to learn and adapt to the changing business environment. I want to encourage you to reach out to consultants such as myself in order to help you design and implement changes in your dealership.

I truly hope that this book will help you become a more effective general manager and lead your organization to its best possible performance. Remember selling cars is both an art and a science. Good luck!

35
REFERENCES

GOOD LEADERS SURROUND themselves with a talented team. You need to think of your vendors as team members because their product/service will help your dealership succeed. Below is the list of vendors that have a great product/service and do the right thing.

DMV Services—50 State DMV:

Automotive, recreational vehicle, motorsport and vessel dealerships throughout the United States rely on 50 State DMV's team of professionals to understand the complexities of processing out-of-state transactions. Individuals on our team have years of experience with dealerships in positions ranging from sales to finance to title and registration processing. Our goal in serving every dealership is to help increase efficiency, save time and enhance the customer experience.

Pay-Per-Click—Netembark, LLC:

Netembark LLC, a full service Omnichannel Marketing Company providing results driven strategies to Auto Dealers since 2009. Netembark LLC is powered by an insights-engine that uses a proprietary marketing automation system that allows dealers exceed their expectations among their competition. As a certified Google Premier Partner and Facebook Marketing Partner, we to lead the industry with implementation of innovative technology and digital advertising strategies for the automotive market.

Dealership Compliance—Total Dealer Compliance:

Total Dealer Compliance provides onsite compliance audits and online compliance training for all departments (Sales, BDC, F&I, HR, IT, and Fixed Ops). Establishing a comprehensive compliance program will help your dealership increase customer satisfaction, enhance employee morale while reducing liability associated with finds and penalties for unethical and non-compliant behavior.

F&I Ancillary Products Provider—AutoXcel:

AutoXcel provides a variety of Finance and Insurance ("F&I") products to automotive dealerships for their sale to consumers. AutoXcel prides itself on consistent personable service to contract holders, agents and dealers.

Since 2004 AutoXcel has been providing Agents & Dealerships the products and programs they need for their purchasing customers. At AutoXcel, we provide a personal customer experience. Our agents and dealers know that we are always reachable and responsive to their requests and needs within all aspects of the business from sales, claims, accounting and the president himself. AutoXcel invents the new, responds to requests and is resourceful in providing what the customer, dealership and agent needs. At AutoXcel, we take pride in the being the solutions!

Performance Reporting—SALESVision:

SALESVision is a fully integrated, cloud-based performance reporting platform that allows dealers and warranty agents alike to pinpoint underperforming managers, salespeople as well as products by territory, dealer group or individual staff with a single source login, in near real-time. In addition, robust reports can be emailed at pre-determined intervals as desired. We provide DATA THAT DRIVES - performance, accountability, profit and results.

Whistleblower Hotline— DealershipFraudHotline.com

DealershipFraudHotline.com is designed for dealership employees to anonymously report issues and concerns so the dealer principal and other designated persons can conduct an internal investigation. This is service helps car dealers to protects assets, reputation as well as detect and prevent unethical and non-compliant behavior.

Internet Leads—Rodo

At Rodo, we deliver deals, not leads. Rodo is your go-to digital sales partner and the best way to efficiently enhance your sales. Rodo uses proprietary technology to extend the reach of your dealership, putting your inventory in the hands of in-market customers. For customers, Rodo is the fastest, easiest way to lease new vehicles from local dealers, like you. Our dealer support team helps to set up your inventory and pricing on our dealer dashboard. Customers search and see all of your available stock, then choose a vehicle and lease terms. Rodo automatically alerts you when an order is waiting. Verify a customer's documents right on our dashboard, finalize the lease, and approve. Rodo works with dealerships of all sizes, with flexible features that scale with your business. With thousands of dealers signed up already, now is the time to grow your business with Rodo.

F&I Product Provider—IAS

Founded in 1984 and headquartered in Austin, Texas, IAS specializes in developing superior aftermarket programs and F&I solutions. We exceed our clients' expectations by focusing on unique dealership needs to drive increased profitability, consumer knowledge, and satisfaction. Seven customizable solutions are the foundation of our business, including: Ancillary Coverages, Vehicle Service Contracts, Retail Technology, Income Development, Turnkey Reinsurance, Training Institute, and Performance Marketing. One of the largest F&I product providers in the United States, our team includes hundreds of agents who enhance the sales and F&I process for dozens of the top 100 dealer groups.

Key Management—Supra Automotive

Supra Key Systems - since 1955 our unique lock boxes have been on over 1 million automobiles (and 3 million real estate homes) saving hours of employees and customers time. Our keyboxes let your people open every vehicle on your lots with just a key or keypad. We are the choice of every CarMax in the country, every AutoNation USA store, and the world's largest dealership - Roger Penske's Longo Toyota who uses our keyboxes in sales and service. We enable more sales and save time.

Dealer-Owned Prepaid Maintenance—Dealer Maintenance

CUSTOMER RETENTION

Build a customized loyalty program to increase your customer retention rate from 20%-30% to 60% - 80%. Increase your chance of selling them their next vehicle.

CENTRALIZED SYSTEM

Our web based system simplifies contract and claim management and provides valuable data to grow your business.

SUPPORT & TRAINING

We provide onsite training for your sales team and ongoing support to ensure you have everything you need to promote, sell and fulfill your PPM & Loyalty program.

INCREASED PROFIT

Watch your service department revenue grow and thrive. Get paid to service your customers better than ever before.

Accounting Firm—Rosenfield &Co, PLLC

Rosenfield & Co, PLLC is a full service accounting firm offering Tax, Attestation and Consulting Services tailored specifically to Automotive Dealerships. Their specialized consulting services include Dealership Valuations, Operational Reviews, Merger and Acquisition Services, Litigation Support, Forensic Accounting and Fraud Investigation. Their use of state of the art technology, data extracting capabilities and bench strength sets them apart not only as service providers, but as thought leaders in the Automotive community. To reach one of their experienced team members please email info@rosenfieldandco.com or visit their website at www.rosenfieldandco.com for more information.

Dealership Training—Ted Ings:

Ted Ings is the Executive Director at the Center for Performance Improvement. He is a 4-time NADA (National Automobile Dealers Association) Convention speaker and is one of their highest-rated presenters.

He has successfully implemented dozens of initiatives for OEM's and Total Quality Management processes at thousands of dealerships in North America and around the world, revolutionizing the way vehicles are sold. This makes him an invaluable asset to his clients and they get both the benefit of his vision and his experience.

https://www.centerforperformanceimprovement.com

Direct-to-Consumer VSC Marketing—National Vehicle Protection Services, Inc.:

NVPS offers dealerships an additional revenue stream and partnership upside by protecting their customers from third-party marketing and creating long-term value. No start-up or additional costs, seamless integration with dealership systems, complete outsourcing of customer contact & sales, new channel to increase loyalty & retention, proven track record of success.

Optimally based just outside of St. Louis, in St. Charles, Missouri NVPS is a valued partner to dealer groups, TPAs and agencies. Offering services nationwide since 2007. State of the art corporate office which will house 300 employees. Certified member of the Vehicle Protection Association. All sales and customer service representatives are licensed with Missouri department of Insurance.

Key Control System—1Micro:

For over 20 years, 1Micro has been controlling vehicle keys for dealerships across the world. The KeyMaster is cloud based, engineered for a vehicle key, and takes a 4K image of every user accessing your keys. Use iLot, 1Micro's mobile app to see who has what key, where the key is, and even receive it from the KeyMaster. Additionally, track your vehicle locations with iLot Asset Tracking. Geofence your lot and locate where every vehicle is last parked. You can even perform monthly inventory audits with iLot Inventory Audit. What used to be an all day task now only takes an hour. Let the KeyMaster be your all in one inventory solution!

Lead Generation—Dealer Mobile Leads:

Dealer Mobile Leads provides custom photo overlays on all vehicles in your inventory that gives the customer the call to action to Text for special offers or more information. Great way to build rapport and engage with customer. These are live, exclusive customer initiated leads on a dealership's own inventory. www.dealermobileleads.com

Customer Income Verification—TurboPass:

Problem: Income Misrepresentation Fraud has become a $6B annual problem in automotive and "Stated Income" on credit apps will eventually be eliminated from the industry. It's going to happen the easy way or the hard way. Get ahead of the curve with TurboPass!

Solution: TurboPass is a SaaS-based, patent-pending platform that delivers the truth about a borrower's ability to repay in ways that are easier, faster and more secure for consumers, dealers, and lenders. TurboPass eliminates the hassle and risk associated with traditional document-based verification of income, employment, identity and residence. TurboPass provides trusted direct (bank & credit union) source data that fulfills lenders' need for copies of PDF banks statements, proof of income/proof of employment and other stipulations.

Top 3 Benefits:

1. **Consumers and dealers love a fast sales and finance experience.** Inviting your customers to validate their income and residence using a text link with TurboPass avoids the hassles and time spent gathering, storing,

faxing, emailing, and uploading sensitive documents for buyers, sellers, and lenders.

2. **Dealers get funded faster.** With a growing list of participating lenders, your sub-prime funding delays can become a thing of the past. We've seen our dealers reduce their average CIT days from 3 -10 days to down to a few hours and even minutes when using TurboPass.

3. **Red-Flag risks are drastically reduced.** TurboPass keeps sub-prime "stips" digitally and securely stored for viewing by only the parties that need to know. No more sensitive paper documents flowing through your busy sales location from department to department. Managers and lender partners can easily view the information needed to complete their tasks with confidence and speed.

- Text TURBO to 59262
- https://www.nostips.com

Digital Retail—AutoFi:

AutoFi's digital retail solution is transforming the way cars are bought and sold. Customers can evaluate price, structure their deal, value trade-ins, include protection plans, and select a car conveniently from a mobile device or in-store. Interactive tools capture the entire shopping experience to better engage with your customers and convert them to happy customers. We're the only platform with full-spectrum lender integration and real-time lender decisions. Shoppers become buyers in a fast, convenient, and transparent way improving retention and profitability.

Recruiting Technicians—Find A Wrench

Find A Wrench is a recruiting firm focused on finding Technicians for Dealerships all across the United States. We currently offer three different services aimed at helping shops locate, recruit and retain Techs. The first being our Full Service Recruiting program, which is very similar to a traditional recruiting firm. The biggest difference is that we are completely niche focused and offer extremely competitive rates. Our second offering is our ASR Program. The ASR stands for Assisted Self Recruiting and is aimed at helping Dealerships develop a proactive recruit and retain strategy. This is a month by month service that is aimed at building your pipeline of potential Technician candidates, putting strategies in place and giving you tools to execute the strategy. This has quickly become our most popular offering and offers a lot of value as compared to what you will pay. Lastly, we have a job board focused on Technicians. Like other job boards, you can post your jobs to get visibility to your posting. There are a few different options to choose from in terms of pricing, including a free option. Find out more about Find A Wrench and our offerings by going to FindAWrench.com!

Artificial Assistant—Conversica

Conversica is a true Artificial Intelligence solution that helps augment the sales process. Every lead is important and maintaining a perfect follow up process is critical to the dealerships success. Conversica's solution isn't just limited to the auto industry with customers ranging from the NBA to Sprint.

Advertising Agency—RAM Group

RAM Group and Companies is a high-touch, highly consultative, automotive agency that specializes in both digital and traditional advertising.

We're lucky enough to work with the #1 & #3 Lexus stores in the country (Lexus of Pembroke Pines and Lexus of North Miami), 2 of the top 10 Hyundai stores, 1 of the top 10 Mazda stores, a top 10 Honda store, plus many more - including the #1 Digital Dealer which happens to be the #1 CDJR store in the country (Dave Smith Motors) Hendrick Automotive, Southeast Toyota and more. We manage the following services for our clients:

- SEM
- SEO
- Social Advertising (with Advanced Audience Management)
- Organic Social Posts & Management
- Video Adverting (with Advanced Audience Management)
- Display Advertising (with Advanced Audience Management)
- OTT / Connected TV
- BDC Consulting
    - Appointment setting conversions / Appointment show conversions
- Branding, Retailing
- All integrated media buying
    - Radio, print, SEM, SEO, Pandora, (Based upon your DMS / Polk True market report) and data Science
- Design & Integrate all in-bound marketing & out-bound marketing
- In-House Hispanic marketing department
- Quarterly website Evaluation
- Design & build and launch all eBlast include in fee
- Build out web panels for website and Hang all included in fee

- Email shops store – For content, time response, and spelling
- Email shop competitors for pricing for marketing comparison
- Custom solutions based on forensic research
- Full compliance Dept Factory/ State
- In House co-op Dept that we submit Pre /post

Recently we were named by Facebook as Top 5 Automotive Social Agency in the USA.

Service Retention—SmartTech

SmartTerm will automatically popup on the service advisor when a member of your program is pulled up in your DMS. SmartTerm instantly loads the benefits you have chosen in your custom built program.

- Turnkey Handling of Rewards/Points Programs with Customized Accounts
- Used Vehicle Program to Double Your Retention
- ToyotaCare and Other Manufacturer Initiatives Tracking and Incentive Program
- Create and Track Pre-Paid Maintenance Programs
- Preload Dollars to Drive Behavior in Service and Sales
- Track Your Oil Club Program, Buy 4, Get the 5th Free
- Mileage Driven Upsell Offers Help Advisors Close Additional Work
- Points Used as a Closing Tool During the Sales Process Instead of Discounted After

- Rewards Statement Delivered Quickly and Easily on Every Visit
- Enroll New Customers by Simply Adding an Op Code
- Seasonal Member Offers
- No Internet Look-Up for Advisors, Customers Don't Need to Carry Cards, SmartTerm toolbar Automatically Pops Up with Customer Information

Schedule your dem0—866-4LOYALTY www.4Loyalty.com

Direct Mail and Email Marketing – Premium Productions

Premium Productions is a national leader in automotive direct mail and email marketing. We are celebrating our 20th year of delivering consistent positive results for our customers. Contact us for your no charge market analysis.

Premium Productions,Inc.
premium123.com
1-800-960-5405
Mikeo@premium123.com

Customer Retention—Dealership for Life

Dealership for Life was started in 2004 to help dealers achieve superior customer retention in their market place. Dealership for Life is the number one provider of why buy here, why service here programs in the United States. Blending multiple lifetime programs with proprietary software, they have created a seamless administration process that achieves state of the art results.

A creative blend of individualized customer websites, customer centric apps, digital marketing, and a world class rewards program allows the dealer to have real time interaction with everyone in their data base on a daily basis. Customer loyalty is the Holy Grail of any business and no one does it better than Dealership for Life.

Contact information:
Paul Healy, paul@dealershipforlife.com
Jack Garrity jack@dealershipforlife.com

Dealership for Life
210 North Main St.
Boonesboro, MD 21713
1-800-717-4900

Digital Marketing—Auto Ad Builder

Auto Ad Builder is a full service automotive digital marketing and branding firm. We help car dealers improve their online presence in order to receive more targeted traffic which yields more relevant leads that convert much higher than third party leads, ultimately leading to more sold cars. Unlike our competitors, we are hands on and actually know about automobiles and the trends in the industry. Find us at AutoAdBuilder.com or Call us at 347-495-9688

Equity Mining — Dealer Wizard

Dealer Wizard is a fully automated, intuitive equity mining solution. We are certified through all the major DMS providers and multiple OEM's. Between the simplicity, our automation and full support from the account managers, Dealer Wizard has been proven to protect the dealers most important assets—their owner base. Our proprietary technology automatically analyzes the full scope of your DMS 24/7 and alerts you to owners with the highest probability of repurchasing. We have the intelligence and tactics in place to surpass internal and monthly OEM sales objectives.

Digital Retailing and Inventory Management— MAX Digital

MAX Digital is known in the inventory space for their FirstLook suite that pioneered retail performance analytics. Today they offer a much broader set of products that cover the full retail process from acquiring the cars most likely to sell in your dealership to providing the omnichannel experiences to sell them. What is unique about their approach is the level of consumer research and partnership. They will typically go deep into the process with one or two large groups with a focus to significantly outperform available options. Products aren't launched until they are proven in market. From better managing vehicle content accuracy with MAX Ad and MAX Digital Showroom to MAX My Trade which naturally drives lower valuation through guided customer collaboration, each product is road tested against competitive solutions to deliver a superior return. Early products are not as attractive as their current innovations, but all leverage a solid data platform continues to set the standard in the business and a common mission to deliver proven results.

Dealership Buy/Sell Broker—Lasser Advisory Services

Strategic Planning for Automobile Dealers:

- Place an approximate value on the business assets and goodwill;

- Place an approximate value on the property, or existing leases, that are associated with the business;

- Seek buyers looking to augment their portfolio;

- Create a 'term sheet' that outlines what has been agreed to between a seller and buyer, before turning the transaction over to the respective attorneys;

- Work closely with existing dealers as they transition from the retail automobile business to something else; i.e., I provide support and solitude for dealers during what is often a difficult, emotional time.

Document Management—Dealer Scanning

Provides car dealerships with a customized scanning unit to scan repair orders, deal jackets, parts invoices, rental agreements & vendor invoices.

Selling and servicing cars makes money. People shuffling documents does not!

Searching for repair orders or deal jackets should not be a treasure hunt. A great deal of time and resources are spent searching through paper documents in an attempt to find what is needed. Paperwork can take up a significant amount of space, and this requirement will only get bigger as the number of documents grows.

Paper documents are subject to the threat of natural disasters like floods or fires.

Dealer Scanning helps dealerships increase productivity by removing physical paper storage and archiving and turning them into digital easy to search pdf copies.

DealerScanning.com

THANK YOU FOR READING!

PLEASE REACH OUT IF YOU HAVE ANY QUESTIONS, NEED HELP OR JUST WANT TO TALK ABOUT CAR BUSINESS.

max@maxzanan.com
917-903-0312

www.ingramcontent.com/pod-product-compliance
Lightning Source LLC
Chambersburg PA
CBHW070651220526
45466CB00001B/391